Courageous & Authentic Leadership

Christina M. Gullo, MBA, MSW, SPHR, SHRM-SCP

Copyright © Christina M. Gullo 2024

All rights reserved. In accordance with U.S. Copyright Act of 1976, the scanning, uploading, and electronic sharing of any part of this book without permission of the publisher constitute unlawful piracy and theft of the author's intellectual property. No part of this book may be reproduced in any form by any electronic or mechanical means (including photocopying, recording or information storage and retrieval) without permission in writing from the author or publisher. Thank you for your support of the author's rights. For bulk or wholesale orders, please contact us admin@richterpublishing.com.

Book Cover Design: Richter Publishing with stock art from RF123.com

Editors: Selena Mouzon, Austin Hatch & Abigail Bunner

Additional Contributors: Tara Richter

Publisher: Richter Publishing LLC www.richterpublishing.com

ISBN-13: 978-1-954094-52-9 Paperback

DISCLAIMER

This book is designed to provide information on leadership only. This information is provided and sold with the knowledge that the publisher and author do not offer any legal or medical advice. In the case of a need for any such expertise, consult with the appropriate professional. This book does not contain all information available on the subject. This book has not been created to be specific to any individual's or organization's situation or needs. Every effort has been made to make this book as accurate as possible. However, there may be typographical and/ or content errors. Therefore, this book should serve only as a general guide and not as the ultimate source of subject information. This book contains information that might be dated and is intended only to educate and entertain. The author and publisher shall have no liability or responsibility to any person or entity regarding any loss or damage incurred, or alleged to have incurred, directly or indirectly, by the information contained in this book. You hereby agree to be bound by this disclaimer or you may return this book within the guarantee time period for a full refund. In the interest of full disclosure, this book may contain affiliate links that might pay the author or publisher a commission upon any purchase from the company. While the author and publisher take no responsibility for the business practices of these companies and or the performance of any product or service, the author or publisher has used the product or service and makes a recommendation in good faith based on that experience. All characters appearing in this work have given permission. Any resemblance to other real persons, living or dead, is purely coincidental. The opinions and stories in this book are the views of the author and not that of the publisher.

FOREWORD

At the risk of sounding mellow dramatic, if you stay in leadership long enough, you will eventually reach a crossroads. A moment that will be career defining. A moment when your courage and authenticity will be challenged. A moment that, once passed, will tell everyone who you really are.

After 25 years in the C-suite, leading organizational turnarounds, and managing the people & culture integration of multiple mergers, I have faced such a moment, and can say with complete confidence that leading with courage and authenticity comes at a cost. But, as we say in Florida, "The juice is worth the squeeze!".

When I think of the person most qualified to tackle this topic, Christina Gullo is at the top of my mind. I had the privilege of standing next to her when she had her moment at the crossroads, and I learned that she lives by a set of values that inform every decision and interaction involving the people she leads. I learned that Christina was exactly who she told me she was. After reading this book, you will owe her a debt of gratitude for courageously and authentically pulling back the curtain on her leadership journey; enabling you to benefit from the lessons she has learned.

~ Tony Moore
Culture Architect, Author, Keynote Speaker, Recovering HR Executive

DEDICATION

To my amazing husband, John Mueller, who without his support and coverage at home, I would not have been able to do what I did at the Villa. And to my daughter, Alexandra Paulus, who sometimes had to sacrifice time spent with me due to my job responsibilities, but even at the age of five when I began, knew the important work I was doing was impacting other lives. And to my supportive coaches and mentors, especially Carolyn Portanova, Mary Burkhardt, and Tony Moore, thank you for helping me succeed. Lastly, to my parents, Frank Gullo Jr. & Kathleen Gullo. Mom, for setting an example of a working mother, providing love and structure, and allowing me to travel with my Godmother every summer. Dad, thank you for teaching me how to work hard and not to procrastinate. You taught me to take risks and how to have a great work ethic amongst so many other things. And to the team at the Villa for stepping up and delivering amazing results, even during momentous change.

Shannon, Patrick, John, Christina, Alex and Bella the sheltie.

Table of Contents

ACKNOWLEDGMENTS 12
INTRODUCTION 13
1 A PERSONAL JOURNEY 17
2 MOVING INTO CEO ROLE 29
3 UNEXPECTED JOURNEY 41
4 NAME CHANGE 47
5 SANCTUARY MODEL 54
6 BUILDING A TEAM 62
7 STRATEGIC TRANSFORMATION & DIVERSITY, EQUITY, INCLUSION, AND BELONGING 67
8 LEADING THROUGH A PANDEMIC 75
9 DECIDING WHEN TO EXIT 83
10 MY FATHER'S STORY 89
FINAL THOUGHTS 100
ABOUT THE AUTHOR 105

ACKNOWLEDGMENTS

For my wonderful team at the Villa who led courageously with me, trusted the unknown, and took risks together. We all grew with each other on this journey.

Ribbon cutting at one of the many new programs at Villa of Hope

INTRODUCTION

Most people cannot wait to finally be in a leadership position. If you're a leader, then you've made it. However, leadership is one of the hardest and yet can be one of the most rewarding positions. Seeing people you lead, develop, and grow, both professionally and personally, is amazing to watch. A healthy leader guides others by providing a safe space for discussing fears, concerns, and dreams. Good leadership development comes from the inside, not just from training or webinars. It takes a healthy ego, self-awareness, emotional intelligence, courage, and grit. It is not for the faint of heart, but if done right, it can be the most powerful partnership. Many leaders are uncomfortable admitting they don't have all the answers, especially in the non-profit sector. This can be challenging due to factors beyond your control. This book offers an honest perspective on what leadership truly entails and what it means to be an authentic leader, especially in turbulent times.

What is a leader? The Oxford English Dictionary defines it as, "The person who leads or commands a group, organization, or country." So basically, anyone can lead, but can they do it well? Do they need any qualifications? Leadership is an essential aspect of any organization, and it is the key to success. A leader plays a vital role in guiding and motivating their team towards achieving common goals. Every organization needs not just a leader, but an *authentic* one. The concept of authentic leadership has gained significant attention in recent years, as organizations are striving for ethical and sustainable practices.

Authentic leadership refers to a leadership style that focuses on building genuine relationships with followers, promoting transparency and honesty, and staying true to one's values and beliefs. It is a leadership approach that emphasizes self-awareness, emotional intelligence, relatability, and moral reasoning.

One of the key characteristics of an authentic leader is their ability to be appropriately vulnerable. They are not afraid to show their weaknesses and admit when they make mistakes or do not know the answers. This vulnerability allows them to connect with their followers on a deeper level, creating a sense of trust and transparency within the team.

Moreover, authentic leaders are known for their high levels of emotional intelligence. They are not only aware of their own emotions but also understand how to manage and regulate them effectively. This enables them to empathize with their followers and create a positive work environment that promotes well-being. As a mentor always reminded me "as the leader, you are among the people, a part of the emotions, but not of it" As soon as we as leaders become of it, we lose our ability to lead.

In addition to this, an authentic leader is guided by a strong set of values and beliefs. They do not compromise on their principles, even in the face of challenges or tough decisions. This consistency in behavior helps to build safety and trust within the team and creates a sense of purpose and direction for the organization.

Furthermore, authentic leadership promotes ethical practices and responsible decision-making. These leaders are conscious about their impact on society and strive to make ethical choices that align with their values. They also encourage their followers to do the same, creating a culture of integrity and accountability within the organization.

Overall, this is an important aspect of effective leadership. It helps to build strong relationships and trust between leaders and followers where the environment is collaboratively crafted, created, and nurtured within organizations. As the world continues to evolve and face new challenges, the need for authentic and courageous leaders becomes even more crucial.

My goal is to share my story of how I implemented these strategies and made a positive impact on different teams, organizations, and society as a whole. I hope together we can all do better and strive to be more authentic and courageous in our everyday lives.

Me on the front porch of the house my dad built, and which I grew up in.

1

A PERSONAL JOURNEY

I grew up in Mt. Morris a small rural town in western New York. It had a population of approximately 2,000 people, predominantly white. It was a safe place to raise a family. We never locked our doors, and the keys were often left in our car. Everyone knew each other and would wave hello to passing cars. I was an only child who grew up on my father's family farm. At a young age, I woke early to feed the calves. After school I would retrieve eggs from the coop, and help my dad in the field, all before doing homework.

As a young girl, I never had much time to just be a kid, because there never seemed to be a time when I was not helping on the farm, or around the house. As a family, we never took a vacation in the summer, like many of my friends, as summer was the busy time. The animals needed to be cared for and the crops harvested. Cutting hay was a hot and sweaty job; it was also weather dependent. If the hay was cut and it rained before we could get it baled, the rows would need to be turned and dried prior to baling it. We could not procrastinate and put things off because we were tired, or because it was hard. Our family depended on the revenue from the farm, and the animals depended on us. This tough work schedule instilled a strong work ethic and a sense of responsibility in me, that I would use later in life, even if it wasn't in the barn or fields.

My grandparents lived nearby, so I was allowed to ride my bike to their house for dinner on occasion, and then would hang out with them to watch Family Feud. Their house was the place I could go to relax, and just be a child. My grandmother taught me how to cook, something I still enjoy today. My grandmother also instilled some tradition into our lives, like sharing meals together, having picnics and gatherings out near the pond, special holiday foods and Italian cookies, and made sure we spent time as a family, since we all worked so much.

In addition to working on the farm, my mother obtained her insurance agent certification and worked full-time for an agency. My dad loved working on the land, as his family had for generations before him, and it was his passion. My dad was also a certified contractor, and he built the house I grew up in. My mom wanted a more normal life, more children, and the ability to take vacations, but one child was enough for my dad, and he loved the life of a farmer. My mom supported my dad's ambitions, but this was always a sore point.

I was not the best student in school, often getting C's and the occasional A or B. My school counselor didn't encourage me to go to college, in fact he said I "should look at secretarial positions." However, during my high school years, I spent time with my godmother and cousins. They lived in Rochester, and my godmother was a high school history teacher. Every summer I would visit her for a few weeks. She would take me shopping, to Rochester Red Wings games, and I traveled with her over summer breaks. She and her sisters had attended a nearby community college, and they greatly influenced my decision to go there too. My parents were supportive of me, but they did not expect me to go to college, nor did they think it was necessary. I would be the first in my family to obtain a college degree. However, my dad, who offered very little in the way of parenting advice, often repeated one piece of advice throughout my childhood - "be sure to be able to take care of yourself financially; you never want to depend on someone else as you never know what could happen". And since my dad shared few words of wisdom, this one stuck with me.

I first chose liberal arts and attended Monroe Community College in Rochester. I received my associates degree in 1990. During those two years, I fell in love with psychology, so I transferred to SUNY Geneseo where I graduated with a Bachelors in 1992. At this point I was not sure if I should go back to school for a master's in counseling or social work. When I do not have answers or need more information, I talk to people in the field or those who have related expertise and ask for help and feedback. Many times, these contacts lead to other people who also could offer advice or share experiences. This is my mantra, and it has served me well.

The people I asked advised me to get my master's in social work since it was more marketable. In five years, I could have my own private practice and bill for insurance. So, I enrolled in a master's program with that exact goal in mind. I earned my master's degree in social work (MSW) and my family was just thrilled. This was a huge accomplishment. As mentioned before, I was the first to attend college on both sides of my immediate family - parents & grandparents, and then went on to get a master's degree! My parents did not even really understand why I needed to do this, but I knew I had to.

After I earned my master's, I moved back to Rochester and started working for a non-profit, Catholic Family Center. At this community-based program, my eyes were opened to systematic and institutional racism for the first time. I saw how challenging the system was for the people I was trying to help. I was only 23 at the time. I always say, the people in the programs taught me way more back then than I probably helped them. This exposure led me to an interest in program development. At this point in time, I realized I did not want to do counseling for the rest of my life. I was not sure exactly what I wanted to do, but I knew I wanted to help people through impacting change – system wide change.

One of the systemic problems I learned that first opened my eyes was generational wealth. According to the Center for American Progress,

Black households' wealth amounts to 22.5% of white households' wealth (March 19, 2021). Right here begins a barrier to better school systems, access to tutors, certification in a skilled trade, college, and ultimately higher paying jobs, later impacting the ability to buy a home and save for retirement.

In the same vein, healthcare in these groups is substantially impacted, if it is received at all. To be eligible for benefits and to attend appointments, transportation is critical. For most families I had experience with, that means the bus system, which entails multiple stops, and can also mean bringing kids along without childcare.

The families I worked with, more often than not, had a parent incarcerated. This occurs due to a number of reasons, two of which are: traffic tickets (Data point: people of color are more likely to be pulled over and three times more likely to have their cars searched than white drivers), and possession of illegal drugs, mostly marijuana at that time (Data point: police arrest black Americans for drug crimes at twice the rate of whites, according to federal data, despite the fact that whites use drugs at comparable rates). These single-family households are without a parent and without additional income.

Most of the time, these data points are driven by unconscious biases defined as social stereotypes about groups of people that individuals form outside their own conscious awareness. This happens through our own life experiences and how each of us then may organize the world based upon social information.

I observed these circumstances while I worked at the Catholic Family Center for a total of 16 years. I first started out as a social worker and did that for two years. Then I moved up to a supervisor of General Preventive Programming. Still community based, but with a team and with program development opportunities. In 1997, I became the Human Resources Coordinator. At the time, my organization had an HR position open, so I applied for it and sold myself on my experience as an employee and supervisor, promising that I could learn HR regulations. I wanted to impact the culture, and I got hired for the job! I enrolled in a master's level HR class and learned all I could. My parents and other people in my life were shocked because I had spent money on a master's in social work, and now I was taking a title and a pay cut to work in Human Resources. But I learned valuable lessons about leadership, benefits, performance management, and culture, and eventually I was promoted up the ranks to VP of Human Resources.

After being in Human Resources for 7 years, earning a certification in HR, and being part of the Executive Team, the President/CEO of Catholic Family Center was discussing succession planning, and I began to consider leading an organization. I started thinking about returning to college again to fill in the gaps of my knowledge.

When I worked for the President/CEO of Catholic Family Center, she genuinely cared about people, fostered a transparent and open culture, and made people feel safe. She made sure to listen to people, to communicate regularly, and to live by the values of the organization.

Deciding on my "why" to lead an organization was clear - it wasn't for the title or power, it was about having the ability to create a positive culture, make the right changes and decisions, and impact people. Not just those we have the privilege to serve, but our staff.

In thinking about my knowledge gaps, I wanted education in marketing, strategy, and finance, and that desire influenced me to get my MBA at Rochester Institute of Technology. I attended classes every other weekend for 15 months – all day Friday and Saturday even though my daughter was nine-months old when I began. It was difficult to be away from her, but a mentor at the time gave me advice: "she was so young, she wouldn't really remember it and the older she became, the harder it would become for me." We often don't believe we are capable of handling so much or that we are ready for such challenges, but when we dig deep and follow our gut, we can achieve remarkable things. It's important to trust your intuition and to be open-minded about everything. It was hard to believe that the girl who once wasn't good at school, would have two master's degrees, and even crazier, a degree in business!

Shortly after graduation, and after eleven years of marriage, a three-year old daughter, and counseling, my then husband and I decided to divorce. Of course, none of us marry with the idea we will divorce; however, I do believe that we are each in control of our own growth and development as people. In relationships, that growth (or lack of) either enhances the relationship and makes each other better, or it becomes stagnant and not fulfilling.

I refused to watch my life unfold like my parents, and believed it to be better for my daughter to have a happy, successful and engaged mom, even if it meant through a co-parenting model. During this period of collaborative divorce, I was repeatedly grateful for my father's advice of: "be sure to be able to take care of yourself" - I was financially independent, had a career and could care for my daughter without any dependency on someone else. This independence is powerful.

Alexandra and I at my work group for the MBA program

Changing Career Path

In 2010, I became the Chief Operating Officer at Catholic Family Center. I had now worked at the agency for 16 years. In my first meetings with my direct reports, I expressed how uncomfortable and strange it was to have this new position, because several of them played a significant role in my career development, and some had even supervised me. I explained to them that in my role, I wanted to remove the usual paradigm and instead view us as partners. I asked questions like, "Have you considered this?" rather than telling them what to do. It's about our shared goals and effectiveness, and if we're not meeting our goals, then a new approach should be considered. The people who were once my supervisors were now calling me *their* supervisor. I gave them credit and emphasized that I saw my role as removing barriers for them. From there, it was all about earning their trust through actions, not just words. You can say anything, but it's how you support them, follow through, and genuinely care that matters most. I didn't have a leadership coach at the time, but I read every leadership book I could!

Leadership Lessons from Mary Kay

For three years in the late 1990's and early 2000's, I worked part-time as a Mary Kay consultant. I liked the skincare and make-up, so I thought it would be fun. There were valuable leadership lessons there. I even earned a red Pontiac Grand Am. In order to get the pink Cadillac, you had to be a director. But regardless, it was a memorable experience for me.

Mary Kay Ash was an American businesswoman and entrepreneur who founded Mary Kay Cosmetics in 1963. She had a vision of empowering women and providing them with an opportunity to grow as entrepreneurs, regardless of their background or education. Through her company, she created a unique business model that fostered the development of individual leadership skills.

As a leader herself, Mary Kay believed in leading by example. Her leadership style was based on empowering her employees, recognizing their capabilities, and encouraging them to reach their full potential. She also believed in the power of recognition and rewards to motivate her team members.

Through her company, Mary Kay created a culture that promoted personal development, strong work ethics, and excellence – all essential qualities of a successful leader. Her belief in continuous learning and self-improvement also paved the way for leadership development programs within her company.

Today, Mary Kay Cosmetics continues to excel as a leading beauty brand, with a strong emphasis on developing and nurturing future leaders. Aspiring leaders can learn valuable lessons from Mary Kay's approach to leadership, such as the importance of empowering others, having a clear vision, and fostering a positive work culture.

The five foundations of the successful Mary Kay business model:
1) **Passion:** love what you do.
2) **Purpose:** be a part of something greater than yourself. The Power of We.
3) **Preparation:** learn something new every day.
4) **Perseverance:** don't quit before the blessing.
5) **Personal Accountability:** accept personal responsibility for your life.

Doors Open, Even When You're Not Ready

I was in my new role for only about eight months when another new position opened at a different agency. It was for a President/CEO. It was an exciting idea, but I was not sure I was ready for that just yet in my professional or personal life as my daughter was four years old. I had acquired a lot of good experience at my current company, yet I was 39 years old. I felt I needed more time in my COO role first before considering a CEO position.

However, I decided to look at it for a couple of different reasons. For one, Catholic Family Center was very diversified in their programs. They did everything from helping infants through adulthood, homeless and housing, refugee resettlement, substance use, and aging services. I always thought it was very hard for us to state what our true expertise was, what we were *really* good at, because it was so broad. It was intriguing for me to be able to go to an organization that was specifically at that time focused only on kids and families.

The second reason was, I watched the current President/CEO struggle with many different obstacles within her role. She was planning her retirement in a couple of years, and I knew she was grooming me to possibly take over her position. She had shared with me the difficulty in her position due to the legal connection to the Diocese of Rochester. There were many times that the Diocese would have a directive and the agency would need to follow it, even though it might not have aligned with our values. A good example of that at the time was health insurance coverage for birth control pills. They had removed it from the health insurance policy, and we had to then share with our employees that it was "carved-out." Ultimately, we found a solution where women could still get them if they were prescribed this medication from their doctor. Nonetheless, this example was one of the challenges with being under the umbrella of the Diocese when leading an organization and trying to retain staff. St. Joseph's Villa, where the new opportunity was, had separated themselves from the Diocese in the 1970's.

The final third and final reason I decided to apply to this CEO role was my colleague/friend. We went out for breakfast, and she told me more about the Villa and their operation. I was nervous and I did not think I was ready for the leap. She encouraged me and said, "No, you are ready! You need to apply!"

Chapter Tips:
1) Take risks and follow your gut.
2) Let others believe in you and help you.
3) Listen and learn from others who have a different lived experience.
4) Don't be afraid to change your path, even when others, including societal expectations, disagree.

Me with the red Pontiac Grand Am from Mary Kay

To the love of my life. How blessed our life becomes when we move on from situations where we are unhappy, and we let go of others' opinions.

2

MOVING INTO CEO ROLE

The interview process was interesting. I had about four 1:1 interviews with the search committee members, then the entire committee together, and two more with the management team, which was more of a meet-and-greet. I applied in May and interviewed throughout the summer, receiving the job offer the week I was getting married in August 2010, and I began my new position on November 1st, 2010.

Now a newlywed of three-months, with a move to a new home I built with my husband, and my daughter adjusting to kindergarten in a new school district - to say I already had a lot of changes in my life going on was an understatement. And little did I know, more were coming.

There wasn't a robust leadership development culture at this organization. Strangely, everyone knew the internal candidate wasn't ready for the CEO job, but everyone went through the motions instead of having a direct and transparent conversation with this person. When I arrived in my new position as President/CEO, there had been a leadership team of four white men in place for over two decades. They had been running things quite successfully. The Villa generated significant revenue because it primarily provided residential care for kids. During that era, residential was prevalent because there were limited community-based programs for children. Kids would stay in residential treatment for 2-3 years, attending school onsite. Often, they would transition from residential care to group homes and then apartment programs. It was designed for kids with conduct disorders; those skipping school, running away, or engaging in minor crimes like shoplifting or minor drug offenses. They often ended up in family court rather than criminal court. Judges would try various interventions like involving the Boys and Girls Club or assigning a juvenile probation officer. If the youth's behaviors didn't improve, they'd end up back in front of the family court judge who might decide to send them to residential treatment.

Families could choose where to send their children and that's when some came to St. Joseph's Villa. They would live there in cottages with around 12 other boys or girls. Back then, treatment was often behavior-based and there wasn't enough focus on underlying issues like mental health trauma, drug abuse, or abuse in the family. The goal was to reintegrate them back into their homes, but some stayed in residential treatment if they didn't have a safe home to return to. Eventually, they could move to a group home, which offered more freedom and public-school attendance.

The facility's operations were still based on models from the 70s, 80s, and 90s, despite the changing landscape. The organization was originally founded in 1942 as an orphanage under the Diocese of Rochester, but severed ties with the Diocese in the 70s to become its own social services organization. They specialized in residential programming ever since. While the organization functioned successfully for decades, the world was shifting towards community-based care. However, the leadership and Board were slow to adapt. They believed the tide would turn back in favor of residential care. There was also a lack of awareness about the financial challenges the organization was facing.

When I joined, the organization was already maxed out on the line of credit at $3.5 million, had no unrestricted funds, and had limited development efforts. There was a Foundation of about $4M, but it secured the line of credit and, therefore, was unusable. Since the use of the Foundation was not an option, I wasn't sure how we could continue to make payroll as a cash wall was looming. The former CEO's response to this financial crisis was to avoid bringing it to the Board's attention. This was a stark contrast to my experience at Catholic Family Center, where collaboration and transparency with the Board was essential.

To address the crisis, I convened a meeting with the Board Chair and Finance Chair and laid out the situation. They were unaware of the severity of the issue. I recommended bringing in outside help to assess the situation and gain further information quickly. As I delved deeper and proposed necessary changes, both the Senior Vice President of Programs and Vice President of Administration chose to retire. So, I found myself as the new CEO without an Executive Team. Additionally, the Board Chair and Finance Chair agreed that we needed to convene the Executive Committee of the Board to discuss the fiscal crisis, assess our cash flow, refinancing options, and consider staff layoffs. The organization was top heavy with multiple director-level positions in various departments. I presented the facts to the Executive Committee, stating that if they weren't willing to support the necessary changes, I would resign immediately. If they agreed, we could work together to address the crisis, even if it meant mergers or, worst case, closure. I had to deal with all this within six months of accepting the role.

Who To Trust?

I decided to get an executive coach because I needed someone to talk openly and unfiltered with and guide me through this unexpected situation. In a new environment, I had no idea who I could trust. Plus, here I am, a young woman, who had just turned 40 but looked younger than that, walking into the "boys club" trying to lead and direct. I am sure I must have looked unqualified to some.

I was completely exhausted and felt very alone driving home at the end of very long days. There were many moments when I didn't want to deal with the crisis, but every night, in long conversations with my husband while reviewing the day, I was always clear of the next best steps.

I began meeting with all staff and avoided any blaming, shaming, or using names. I focused on what the organization had done well for many years and presented the facts about industry changes, current numbers, and financial realities. It was a brutal process and I had to lay off some long-standing employees, including a nun, which weighed heavily on me.

These people had supported each other and had been together for a long time. We had to say good-bye to about 37 people, and I believe that how you handle such situations is a reflection of your leadership. We had a comprehensive communication plan, and I personally met with each affected individual to explain the reasons and the organization's best chance of survival. It was a long day, but it is important to treat people with dignity and respect. We even had an event to honor those leaving which was an emotional time. This approach may be harder, but I believe it's what courageous leadership entails. Terminating someone's employment is heart-wrenching, but honesty, respect, and open communication can make a difference. I've had to let people go and some later thanked me for the lessons learned and the change, finding themselves much happier on the other side. It's all about explaining why things are happening and treating people with respect, even when they may be angry and upset.

Building Relationships/Trust/Ambassadors

I started meeting with the group of directors that were part of the communication and strategy work, and with others within the organization, so people would get to know me and hopefully feel like I was more approachable. Human services organizations typically have a higher percentage of women, so I think many women were probably excited about me being the new President/CEO. I'm sure some of the men were wondering if I was fit for the role and some people probably thought I was too inexperienced. Being a young CEO meant earning trust and respect was even more important. It was even more challenging because I had to convey that we were facing a crisis, and many were unaware of it before I brought it to their attention. The organization had a patriarchal culture, where they believed they could handle everything without causing stress for employees. And most of the staff rarely had experience or professional relationships outside of the Villa. Therefore, I had to step out to team meetings and deliver brutal facts that were hard for them to hear. There were some people who decided to leave at various times throughout my early tenure because of the changes I started to implement.

Change Management

When you start to make that culture shift, there's a tipping point where more people are on board and excited with it than the people who are uncomfortable or unhappy with the change. When that shift happens, those loudest naysayers lose momentum and start to self-select themselves out of the organization.

There is no denying that change can be uncomfortable and even unsettling for many people. While some may welcome it with open arms, others may resist or even fear it. This aversion to change is not uncommon and has been observed in various contexts, from individuals dealing with personal changes to entire organizations undergoing transformations. A majority of people avoid discomfort.

In a work setting, where people are expected to perform at their best, any changes in the company's structure or processes can cause uneasiness. This is because employees have grown accustomed to a certain way of doing things and any changes may disrupt their workflow and routines. Moreover, changes in a company's culture or values can be particularly challenging for employees who have been with the organization for a long time, as they may feel like their identity within the company is being threatened.

To create a more comfortable environment for people to embrace change, organizations can focus on building a culture that values flexibility, resilience, and open-mindedness. This can be achieved by creating a safe space for employees to voice their concerns, providing support during transitions, and promoting a growth mindset.

Negativity

There was an individual on my team who really believed in the changes and wanted to live it, but she could not align her want, with the reality of her own self-awareness. She would say things in meetings that were way off culture and treated people with poor body language and tone. I had multiple conversations with her, but eventually I told her that her inability to be in alignment with our values was creating too much damage within our environment. She had to leave.

Accountability to values and culture is key to change. Especially for the leader themselves or someone on their team. All employees are watching to see if leadership is acting in alignment with their values. If you have someone on your team who is not, it sends a clear pass to everyone else. A mentor of mine reminded me of the quote "The culture of any organization is shaped by the worst behavior the leader is willing to tolerate."

With change comes resistance and negativity, especially when there are large shifts going on within the establishment. Negativity in the workplace can manifest itself in various forms, such as gossip, complaining, criticism, conflict, and collective disturbances that go underground. It is often fueled by stress, frustration, and lack of communication among leaders and team members.

One of the primary reasons for negativity in the workplace is a toxic work culture. If employees feel undervalued or unsupported by their colleagues or leaders, it can lead to a negative attitude towards work. Moreover, personal issues and external factors can also contribute to negativity in the workplace. Employees are humans with lives outside of work and therefore, their personal stresses can come to work, causing them to be easily agitated or quick to criticize others. It's crucial during big changes that everyone is on the same page and making sure the leaders are having conversations with the staff, so they don't feel left out. They have to feel included and part of the problem-solving team, so they know we are in this together. Some people will never be on board, and they will weed themselves out or will need to be asked to exit, and that's okay. You have to overcome the majority of the negativity and not let it go underground and become a collective disturbance.

Overcoming Negativity

While it may seem daunting, there are steps that can be taken to overcome negativity in the workplace. Here are a few strategies that can help improve the overall work environment and promote positivity:

- **Encourage open communication:** Creating an environment where employees feel comfortable expressing their concerns or frustrations can prevent negativity from festering. At the Villa, one way we did this was by enacting regular Senior Leadership sessions with the Executive Leadership Team and Town Hall meetings for all staff.
- **Promote a positive work culture:** Companies should prioritize creating a positive work culture that values and supports its employees. This includes recognizing and rewarding achievements, providing opportunities for growth and development, and fostering a sense of team among colleagues. At the Villa, I would be the first presenter for New Employee Orientation every other week where I would share the mission, vision, guiding principles, and strategy. Even more importantly, I

would share my personal story, my "why" in being a CEO, listen to why they chose the Villa, and explained my open-door approach.

- **Address issues promptly:** When negativity arises, it's important to address the issue promptly. This can involve having investment conversations with those involved, finding solutions to improve the situation, and setting expectations while moving forward and following up.
- **Lead by example:** As a leader, it's essential to model positive behaviors and attitudes. Your team will take cues from you, so it's important to demonstrate professionalism and positivity in your own actions. Just think about parents and kids. If kids see stress, frustration, anger, or a "sky is falling" mentality from their parents, they will feel that too.
- **Encourage self-care:** Negativity can take a toll on employees' mental and emotional well-being. Encouraging self-care practices like taking breaks, practicing mindfulness, and maintaining a healthy work-life balance can help employees cope with negativity in the workplace. Self-care was a topic area in one-on-one supervisions at the Villa.
- **Provide resources for support:** It's also important to provide employees with resources for support, such as counseling services or employee assistance programs. These resources can help employees manage their emotions and navigate tricky situations. The Villa offered an Employee Resource Representative. They could call this person for any needs both personally and professionally.
- **Foster a culture of feedback:** Regularly seeking feedback from employees can help address any underlying issues and improve the overall work environment. This shows that the company values its employees' opinions and is committed to creating a positive workplace. At the Villa, we did this through Employee Engagement Surveys, quarterly Town Halls, and weekly supervisions.
- **Communicate openly and transparently:** Clear communication is

key to creating a positive work environment. This involves being transparent about company goals, expectations, and changes, as well as actively listening to employees' concerns/questions and addressing them promptly. It is imperative that employees understand what the plan is, how they can contribute to the plan/strategy, and engage in regular communication on progress.

- **Address negativity directly:** If there are specific individuals or situations causing negativity in the workplace, it's important to address them directly. This can be done through constructive feedback, setting clear boundaries, and finding ways to resolve conflicts.
- **Recognize and address burnout:** Negativity can often lead to burnout if left unaddressed. It's important for employers to recognize the signs of burnout and take steps to prevent it, such as promoting work-life balance/integration and offering mental health resources.
- **Encourage inclusivity, diversity and belonging:** A diverse and inclusive workplace can contribute to more ideas and different perspectives, arriving at better decisions. Employers should actively promote diversity and inclusion, listen to the perspectives of all employees, and ensure that everyone feels valued, included, and that they belong. This became a strategic priority for Villa of Hope.
- **Offer opportunities for growth:** Providing opportunities for personal and professional growth can boost employee morale and create a sense of positivity in the workplace. This can include offering training and development programs, mentorship opportunities, and career advancement opportunities.
- **Recognize and celebrate achievements:** It's important to recognize and celebrate the achievements of employees, both individually and as a team. This can boost morale, foster a sense of team, and create a positive work culture. A few examples from the Villa were recognition of service awards, shout outs for behaviors in alignment with values, and employee appreciation events.

- **Promote a healthy work-life balance/integration:** Encouraging a healthy work-life balance/integration can help prevent burnout and promote overall well-being. Employers should offer flexible schedules, remote work options, floating holidays and encourage employees to take time off when needed.
- **Encourage teamwork:** Foster a sense of teamwork and collaboration among employees. This can help build strong relationships, increase productivity, and create a positive work atmosphere. A tool as simple as the Myers Briggs to understand temperament styles and communication styles is great.
- **Provide resources for mental health support:** Employers should provide resources for mental health support such as Employee Assistance Programs (EAPs) and access to therapy. This can help employees cope with stress and other negative emotions in the workplace.
- **Conduct regular check-ins:** Regular one-on-one meetings between managers and employees can provide a space for feedback, address any concerns, and offer support. These check-ins also allow for recognition of accomplishments and provide opportunities for growth and development. At the Villa, I held 1:1 supervisions/check-ins with my direct reports one hour every week and the minimum agency-wide was at least 30 minutes every two weeks. Additionally, I would hold "Coffee with Chris" listening sessions multiple times throughout the year for non-management staff. This gave me an opportunity to answer questions, hear what was top of mind for staff and share information.

Chapter Tips:
1) Be honest about the current climate of the company with everyone and lay out a plan to address the situation.
2) Deliver the hard news yourself.
3) Don't play the blame game.
4) If you have to lay off people, don't delegate that task.
5) Honor the people you do have to let go in a tactful way.
6) Get a professional coach to help you because you need a compassionate ear as well.
7) Face the choice between what is RIGHT and what is easy.

My good-bye party at Catholic Family Center - Carolyn, one of my early mentors.

3

UNEXPECTED JOURNEY

There were Board members that were with the organization for a long time. They were offered 3 three-year terms for a total of nine years, and then most would move to the Foundation Board. The Board's role had been to provide general oversight, and Board committees such as Human Resources and Development did not exist. The Finance Committee met twice a year, first for budget approval and then for the audit. I needed something very different from this Board and the committees. First, we needed a shared understanding and agreement about the Board's role and responsibilities. So, in partnership with my Board Chair, I started working with them to write and approve a detailed job description. We also reduced the Board term to 2 three-year terms for a total of six years. In conjunction with the Nominating Committee, we established a list of skills and expertise we needed and set expectations moving forward regarding committees and meeting schedules. Some Board members decided to leave at that point, saying "this isn't what I signed up for" and voluntarily left. That made it a little bit easier for us so we could recruit new members with fresh ideas and the expertise we needed. There were others the Board Chair spoke with and if they were not on the same page, they were encouraged to exit.

We started seeing existing Board members step up and we began infusing new people on the Board. They consisted of business owners, benefit consultants, the Police Chief, Financial Services, CPA, medical doctor, Human Resources, IT, a former CEO of a not-for-profit, and diversity including people from a range of different social and ethnic backgrounds and genders.

I sought out a referral from a Board member I knew from Catholic Family Center, who worked with the organization JC Jones & Associates, a financial turnaround organization. I called this individual and asked him to send me someone for the Board specific to rebuilding the Finance Committee. He sent me Ted Cordes. He remained with me the entire time that I was at the Villa. When we realized we needed somebody from the outside to come in and act in the CFO role, he came off the Finance Committee and became my interim CFO. Together, Ted and I focused on cash flow, cash wall, P&L development, reducing cost structure, recapitalization, working capital, financial systems, and internal controls.

Through this analysis, it became clear there would be a projected shortfall of $1.1M due to structural operating deficits, a short runway in cash flow, manual processes, underutilization of assets, and room to reorganize the current administrative structure. Overall, the line of credit was projected to climb to $4.0 million by 12/31/12 and it became imperative to put in place a restructuring approach and target 1.1 million expense reduction by 1/5/12. In this cost reduction initiative, 50 positions were eliminated or restructured across all areas. In addition, decisions were made to exit low fit programs, address program deficits, move programs to space we owned, and then begin to plan for mental health programming.

By February 2012, the Villa had turned a corner from crisis management to sustainability and growth. We had opened two new programs, negotiated a rate intensification for residential (including a $506K retro payment), expedited Medicaid reimbursements and improved Accounts Receivable management by $900k. The Villa's overall revenue budget was almost $19 million in 2008 versus $22 million in 2012 and was serving about 2,000 kids and families a year. Ted Cordes acted as my interim CFO for about 4 months and when that work was done, he returned to the Board. He was instrumental in moving the Board forward with a focus on Vision, Mission, Values, new organizational culture, process improvements, technology, restructuring debt, and use of assets.

By March 2012, based on the structural cost reductions and revenue enhancing results achieved, the projected line of credit moved from $4 million to $2.2 million, and Villa was projecting a quarterly operational surplus in January – June 2012. I then began looking for a banking relationship that wanted to partner in moving our strategy forward and was willing to look at refinancing options. After multiple meetings with four different banks, we found a partner who embraced our strategy and believed in our path forward. The Villa was able to refinance a term loan and eliminated the line of credit through a mortgage on the property.

This allowed us to pay off the line of credit, free up the Foundation assets, and invest back into the organization in areas such as programming and infrastructure. These investments included compensation, training, safety, strategic planning, technology, and rebranding.

Board Transformation and Moving Forward

Being able to mortgage the property and pay off the line of credit helped to elevate the Board's role in the transformation, and fostered a new, higher level of involvement. The Finance Committee began meeting monthly and the Nominating Committee began to review Board polices and best practices for governance. This led to a nominating process for the Board, Board orientation and meetings with agendas communicated in advance to committees. Next up was in-depth strategic planning.

Since I did not have an Executive Leadership Team, I chose 10 people across the organization, along with my Board chair, and worked with an external consultant (who also was my Executive Coach) to facilitate the discussions. The process consisted of a look back in history, an environmental scan and SWOT, competitive landscape analysis, and a review of the overall residential capacity nationally, in New York and Upstate, along with development of Mission, Vision, Values and Value Proposition. As each of these areas were completed, the information was shared with full Board and staff to receive feedback, complete tweaks, and get buy in. Finally, we began holding half-day Board Retreats where information was shared, breakout groups formed, generative conversations had, and decisions made.

The final step was in the development of a Strategy Map/Balanced Scorecard with four main perspective areas: Talent & Culture, Internal Processes, Clients, and Value Impact. Each perspective area had clear strategic objectives along with metrics to move the objective forward. This plan was critical in getting all Board and staff on the same page, as well as maintaining a focused lens into the future. Momentum was building and staff were feeling more confident.

One final important piece of the structure that was added during this time was my Executive Assistant, who I hired from my previous role. It is critical that as leaders we have a right-hand person we can trust, who knows how we respond and operate in circumstances and who lives the culture and values being built. Erika Sollie was this for me and the Villa of Hope for my entire tenure. I would never have accomplished all I did without her partnership!

Chapter Tips:
1) Write out clear Board job descriptions/expectations.
2) Find the right people for your team, Board, etc.
3) Use your resources for help.
4) Let go of the past legacy programs if they don't fit your new mission/strategy.
5) Get clear on mission and vision and set strategy plan – be inclusive.

Pride Parade

4

NAME CHANGE

Part of the strategy conversation was that many people still thought we were part of the Diocese, which had not been the case since 1972. Additionally, we were revamping our program models. So, we considered rebranding in 2012, two years into my tenure. We secured a $100,000 grant for strategy planning, which covered most of the work. We collaborated with a local marketing organization and formed a team to operate as a task force.

Joe and Julie Miller - the gentleman who was at one of the first orphanages at the St. Joseph's Villa

Non-profit erases deficit, adopts new name

St. Joseph's Villa has new systems, rebrands itself as Villa of Hope

By NATE DOUGHERTY

Facing a mounting deficit, St. Joseph's Villa implemented a wide-ranging plan in 2011 to cut costs and introduce new systems to better serve the young people who are its clients.

Those changes have helped the non-profit turn what would have been a $1.2 million deficit into a surplus for the current year.

Now the organization is getting a new identity to go with its new approach.

St. Joseph's Villa has adopted a new name, Villa of Hope. Administrators said the need for this new identity became clear during the strategic planning process to address the deficit.

"We were once part of the Diocese of Rochester as an orphanage but left in the 1970s to be come our own stand-alone agency," said Christina Gullo, president and CEO. "We still have a connection to the Sisters of St. Joseph, but we found that when we asked people what they think of when they hear St. Joseph's Villa, the No. 1 response was that we're a religious organization."

While the name St. Joseph's Villa often led people to believe the organization had remained part of the Diocese of Rochester, a survey found that the word Villa in the name carried a strong brand awareness, Gullo said.

The agency plans an event Tuesday to celebrate the new name, bringing in donors and board members along with other stakeholders.

With the new name comes a new logo, one that shows multiple homes representing the different care settings the organization offers in the community. Each of those has a heart in its center, representing the spirit growing inside the organization, Gullo said.

After working through several options for a new name, the agency settled on Villa of Hope, Chairwoman Laurie Baker said.

"When we all came onto that name, it perfectly captures the aim of the organization and that circumstances can get better," Baker said.

Adding the word "hope" was an important step, Gullo noted.

"This is what we're all about," she said, "hope for families that have lost their own, hope for children getting the help that we provide, hope when people are in the darkest tunnels before they get to us."

Villa of Hope also changed its tagline, replacing "Caring for kids in crisis" with "Rebuild, Recover, Renew."

"We felt the old one was very stigmatizing, and now it's strength-based," Gullo said.

The organization itself is stronger now. Various factors, including a drop in occupancy rates, caused revenue to fall from $22 million in 2008 to $19.6 million in 2011.

While revenue fell 15 percent, the organization cut spending by only 10 percent, noted Gullo, who took over in late 2010. This led to mounting deficits that were projected to reach $1.2 million in fiscal year 2012.

Instead the Villa took a deep look at its operations.

"We started really digging into the numbers in terms of where the bleed was coming from, and when we tore it apart, we could see that expenses were not aligned in residential areas," Gullo said.

At the same time, the staff often struggled to meet the needs of young clients.

"It was a perfect storm of financial crisis and a population of kids that were coming to us later in the process," Gullo said. "The staff was really not equipped to deal with the trauma these kids were coming in with."

As a result, the Villa had a 102 percent turnover rate as the young people in the facility did not stay and staff had difficulty with the ones who did.

"We did expense reductions, got an increase for our bed rates and made some structural improvements and consolidated some responsibilities," Gullo said.

Board members used the situation as a chance to work on long-term strategies as it restructured.

"We knew we needed to focus on strategy and transformation and that it could not wait," Baker said. "So simultaneously we worked through our financial struggles and financially planning while also being forward-thinking. A key part was that we knew that we needed a plan to move the organization forward."

As part of the approach, the Villa restructured its long-term debt. During the fiscal crisis it had a $3 million line of credit that had been tapped out to deal with the agency's losses, Gullo said.

After the restructuring, the line of credit was changed to $1.5 million, and it is now used only to cover the ebbs and flows of receivables. There are many days when the credit used is at zero, Gullo said.

Some decisions were difficult, she said. The organization eliminated its eating disorder program, Harmony Place, and had to cut some staff.

To better meet the needs of its clients, the Villa adopted a "sanctuary model." This recognizes the young people who are seeking services have experienced trauma that can be severe; as many as 8 percent have suffered sexual assault and 17 percent physical assault, and those number are higher for youths from areas of high poverty.

The plan uses seven guiding principles to provide a safe place for these young people to learn to cope, Gullo said. To keep track of all of its new initiatives, the organization has implemented a new system of data collection. It will allow it

Reprinted with permission of the Rochester Business Journal.

One committee member named Joe Miller, who was an original resident of St. Joseph's Villa, initially opposed the name change, so I invited him to join the team. Having been a part of the process, research, and hearing the discussions of the task force team, he came to understand, appreciate, and support the change, becoming a strong advocate who helped others to accept the idea. After many iterations, we settled on "Villa of Hope" as the new name, keeping "villa" for its historical importance. The tagline changed from "Caring for Kids in Crisis" to "Rebuild, Recover, Renew" to reflect our expanded services for adults. This was launched through a press conference and staff celebration on April 23, 2013.

It is important to note that before this rebranding, the Villa didn't have an up-to-date website for easy online search results. So, we invested in a redesign and social media marketing for our launch. Before my tenure, there wasn't an electronic health records system. Clients had multiple binders, so we had to digitize everything. This meant an investment in gathering requirements, an RFP process and selection, and implementation of an electronic health care record for each client. Additionally, other than managers, staff didn't have email and there was limited social media presence, or branding. All this was implemented in the first three years. I had to hire a Chief Development Officer, a high-level Marketing Director, and a Director of Information Technology. In 2012, you needed to have someone supporting your technology on site for this size organization.

Importance of Social Media Marketing

Social media marketing has become increasingly important for nonprofits in recent years. With the rise of social media platforms such as Facebook, Twitter, and Instagram, organizations are able to reach a wider audience than ever before. One of the main benefits of social media marketing for nonprofits is its low cost compared to traditional forms of advertising. Nonprofits often have limited budgets and resources, making it difficult to invest in costly marketing campaigns. However, with social media, organizations can create and share content for free or at a minimal cost. This allows them to effectively promote their cause and reach potential donors without breaking the bank.

In addition to its affordability, social media also offers a wide range of targeting options. Nonprofits can use various tools and features on different platforms to reach their desired audience. For example, Facebook allows organizations to create custom audiences based on demographics, interests, and behaviors. This level of targeting enables nonprofits to reach individuals who are more likely to be interested in their cause and therefore more likely to donate.

Social media also makes it easier for nonprofits to engage with their audience and build relationships with potential donors. Through platforms like Twitter and Instagram, organizations can share updates and stories about their impact, as well as interact with followers through comments and direct messages. This helps to humanize the nonprofit and create a personal connection with supporters, making them more likely to become long-term donors.

Moreover, social media marketing allows nonprofits to track their progress and measure the effectiveness of their campaigns. Platforms like Twitter and Facebook offer analytics tools that can provide valuable insights into the performance of posts and ads. This data can help nonprofits make informed decisions about their social media strategy, such as which types of content resonate with their audience, or which platforms are driving the most engagement.

Overall, social media marketing is crucial for nonprofits because it allows them to effectively promote their cause, reach a targeted audience, build relationships with supporters, and measure the success of their efforts. With the increasing presence and influence of social media in our daily lives, it is essential for organizations to utilize these platforms to further their mission and make a meaningful impact in the world.

The Turnaround

The strategy objectives and KPI's were what the Executive Leadership Team lived and led by, and what was used to build a new organizational structure to achieve the strategy. By 2014, the Villa of Hope budget was almost $22 million through the addition of new programs and fundraising. For every one youth in a residential program, the Villa was serving three in community-based programming.

During this time, the Villa invested in a compensation analysis and initiative. All positions were benchmarked, job descriptions updated and graded, and pay ranges were established with an objective to be competitive within the local market. Any positions below the minimum were lifted to meet the pay grade minimum, positions were moved to higher grades and compression was addressed. Along with this investment, the Villa moved from an across-the-board COLA raise on annual anniversary dates to a performance based annual review process.

From an internal process strategy, an electronic medical record platform was implemented, and programs moved from a paper-based process to a system with a clinical and billing function. Due to the shifts made at the Villa, the agency was now well positioned to capitalize on Medicaid redesign programs which fit our portfolio. We were on the path to growth.

Chapter Tips:
1) Include those who oppose new ideas.
2) Create Ambassadors for your brand.
3) Use social media for low-cost marketing.
4) Most often, the hardest thing and the right thing are the same.
5) Invest in your staff – they are your greatest asset.

Cutting the ribbon with my team at the Villa

5
Sanctuary Model

Organizations who work with people with emotional and behavioral disorders face enormous amounts of obstacles and stress. I realized once I came into the Villa, the level of the needs for the youth coming to residential had shifted, and the team members needed knowledge and training on how to effectively work with clients who have mental health needs. It was crucial that our staff have all the resources available to them, so that our agency was educated, successful with treatment, and able to handle the pressures of working in the human services systems.

The kids that were coming in had higher mental health needs and had experienced a lot of abuse/trauma. The kids with lower-level needs were now treated within community-based programs. Our direct care teams did not understand mental health and the effects of trauma on brain development. We began educating the staff about the impact to the frontal lobe of the youths' brain and how that has a direct correlation on impulse control and executive functioning skills. It's interesting that young people's brains are actually smaller when they've experienced trauma.

When you're reminded of a traumatic experience, your amygdala (the emotional and survival center in the brain) goes into overdrive, acting just as it would if you were experiencing that trauma for the first time. Your prefrontal cortex also becomes suppressed, so you're less capable of controlling your fear--you're stuck in a purely reactive state. Meanwhile, trauma also leads to reduced activity in the hippocampus, one of whose functions is to distinguish between past and present. In other words, your brain can't tell the difference between the actual traumatic event and the memory of it. It perceives things that trigger memories of traumatic events as threats themselves. Trauma can cause your brain to remain in a state of hypervigilance, suppressing your memory and impulse control and trapping you in a constant state of strong emotional reactivity.

Most of our teams didn't fully understand this. Therefore, they felt scared when faced with these big behaviors and conflicts and would revert to prior consequence-based methods, which would intensify the situation. Once at this stage, staff would call the police as the situation was out of control.

That first six months after I began working at the Villa, the police were there all the time because staff would just call 911, hoping that just seeing the police would cause the kids to calm down. But instead, it was traumatic for everybody. It was retraumatizing for the youth. The police didn't know how to handle the mental health issues properly either. They would use force, arrest them or God forbid, taser them, which was horrible. I was fortunate to have a wonderful Chief of Police in the town the Villa was part of. He and I worked in partnership to strategize, educate, and create processes to reduce police involvement.

In addition, that's when we started talking about getting help to educate the staff about trauma and the effects of trauma on the brain. This was done in order to give them tools to deal with the mental health aspect of their care. Of course, there's always going to be a group of naysayers or those who want a quick fix. The people working in the cottages felt very unsafe, and rightly so.

I kept holding town hall meetings and had uncomfortable conversations about how they were feeling. All I could say was, I understand why, and this was not going to change overnight, but here are the investments that we're going to make. There were people who then believed that we would follow through on that. And then there was a group of doubters who said, "oh, it's just the flavor of the month", and "we've heard this before". But we did follow through. I did my research and again, through a Task Force team of 25 staff across the organization, The Sanctuary Model℠ was selected, and we began to work with the Institute.

The Sanctuary Model℠ is a holistic approach for change. It promotes safety and recovery from adversity through the active creation of a trauma-responsive community. The Sanctuary Model℠ was founded and developed by Dr. Bloom within an inpatient mental health setting. The Villa is the only Sanctuary certified organization in upstate New York. Its guiding principles are open communication and psychological safety.

The Sanctuary Institute normally would request that two people go to the institute, go through training, and have the two people return to train the rest of the organization. When I was President/CEO, we had three people from the institute come to us in December 2011 and cross-train 50 people throughout the organization. This was totally unheard of because you just didn't do training like that. But I knew we needed a large group of ambassadors trained. Not just a few, ALL of us.

In March 2012, we held a kick-off event at the Villa and between March – June 2012, we trained all 350 employees, including 100% of the Board. In addition, all Senior Leaders, Directors, and Managers received basic supervision/coaching training. It is critical that the people you supervise see you living the guiding principles. Following the training, we developed a Core Team, recognition programs, and began embedding The Sanctuary Model℠ into our policies and practices, job descriptions, supervisory tools, staff meetings, and performance reviews.

Human Resources and I then reviewed all past Performance Reviews. Most staff were given an "outstanding" rating and unfortunately, there was a lack of feedback. We started to put a culture in place of accountability from the job descriptions, and we started having conversations with people about their performance. Some didn't think this was reflective of The Sanctuary Model℠ and we needed to explain that it was in alignment with the open communication and social responsibility guiding principles. As you can imagine, they didn't see that feedback as a gift. If someone isn't performing well, you need to address it and let them know why so they can either change, be trained, or become successful in another position inside or outside the organization.

In The Sanctuary Model℠, psychological safety is not just physical safety, but also moral safety and feeling like you can come to work and make the right decision, do the right thing, and psychologically stay safe. Do I feel safe with my supervisor? Do I feel safe with my coworkers? Do I feel safe to voice what I think without being criticized? Those are important aspects, as well as feeling a commitment to learning and development.

After the model was implemented and was working well, many other establishments wanted to implement it too and asked me what it was I did. The first thing I would ask is if their CEO is on board? If a CEO isn't on board with The Sanctuary Model℠, then it won't work. The CEO needs to be involved, not simply dictating orders from up above. They must be 100% involved with changing the culture of their organization. If they don't live it and breathe it, then it won't work.

So yes, this is a trauma model for how to work with those that we serve, but it's also an organizational change model. The Villa was going through a crisis. There were a lot of changes coming to the staff all at once. So, it gave us a set of guiding principles that the Villa really didn't have before. And those guiding principles were embedded throughout the organization. Now, we had something that we were living by, which included how we work with each other, treat one another and, what we can expect from our co-workers.

Data results during this first year of implementation included: a 51% reduction in police service calls, a 40% increase in planned discharges, and an increase in overall employee satisfaction.

The Definitions of Guiding Principles

The Sanctuary Model℠ shapes the Villa of Hope's organizational performance.

Quality: We provide superior programs, services, and internal processes.

Sustainable Outcomes: We hold ourselves accountable for achieving sustainable outcomes.

Financial Viability: We are good financial stewards.

Youth & Families: We engage from a strength-based perspective.

Collaborative Efforts: We build strong and lasting partnerships, internally and externally.

Internal Process: We maintain clear, strong, and efficient policies and procedures.

Talent & Culture: We empower staff.

Diversity, Equity, Inclusion and Belonging: We believe in the dignity and humanity of all people to reach their full potential.

Seven Commitments of Sanctuary

Villa's Organizational Culture

Social Responsibility: We are accountable, reliable, proactive, positive, and appreciative.

Growth & Change: We innovate, ignite, promote, initiate, and support a change-ready culture.

Democracy: We engage staff, youth, families & volunteers.

Emotional Intelligence: We are caring, compassionate, respectful, balanced, and self-aware.

Open Communication: We demonstrate integrity, honesty, humility, transparency, and vulnerability.

Social Learning: We are courageous, encouraging, committed to seeking and sharing best practices.

Non-Violence: We are committed to physical, social, psychological, and moral/ethical safety.

Chapter Tips:
1) Establish company values and guiding principles and embed them in the organization.
2) Insist on walking the talk from top down – your behavior and day-to-day actions must match your expectations of your team.
3) Do the culture work with your staff, be the example.
4) Hire outside experts to help teach you.

Villa Staff and my Mother-in-Law, JoAnne Mueller – always a support at events such as The Tournament of Hope

6

BUILDING A TEAM

Building a team is an essential aspect of any organization's success, whether it is a for-profit business or a nonprofit organization. A team consists of individuals who bring their unique skills and experiences to the table, working together toward achieving common goals.

We went through probably three different strategy plans when I was there and each of those strategies called for new skill sets and expertise. A hard leadership acknowledgement for folks is the current team you have may not be the right team for the next phase of a strategic plan. This can be a struggle because you have bonded with this team, you're familiar with them. The Board also is not fond of these decisions because they don't like turnover at the Executive Leadership level, but it must happen to achieve the next strategy.

I had to have these tough conversations with people about how impactful they had been, but that I wasn't sure this was the right fit for them going forward. I wanted them to be successful just as much as the organization, but this is very hard for people to hear. People don't want to go and most detest change, but I have found when they finally embrace it, they find themselves happier and end up in a position that's a better fit.

Building a strong team takes time and effort, but the benefits are invaluable. A united, cohesive team can overcome challenges and work towards achieving the organization's goals efficiently. Additionally, a strong team can attract more support from donors, volunteers, and other stakeholders, as they can see the organization's dedication and commitment to its cause.

When building a team for a nonprofit organization, it is crucial to select passionate and diverse individuals who align with the organization's values and reflect the people we are serving at all levels of the organization, especially at the C-Suite. Establishing clear roles and fostering open communication can improve teamwork and collaboration within the group. Recognizing and appreciating each team member's contributions can boost morale and motivation. With a committed and united team, a nonprofit organization can achieve its goals and make a positive impact in the community. Therefore, it is essential to invest time and effort into building a strong team that will drive the organization towards success.

Leadership Development

Not only did my team have their own Executive coach, but I started having the Operational Leadership Team (about 12 people) meet as a group with a leadership coach. When they started meeting for leadership development, we were able to look at succession planning for some of those folks. As part of succession planning, some engaged with individual executive coaching too. Other development happened through certain committees they had an opportunity to be part of, as well as internal trainings. Investment in people is critical.

Leadership is an essential skill for any successful professional. In today's fast-paced and constantly evolving world, being a good leader can make the difference between failure and success. However, the concept of leadership goes beyond just managing people or projects. It involves having a clear vision, strong communication skills, empathy, adaptability, and many other qualities.

Developing these leadership skills takes time, effort, and dedication. It is a continuous process that requires self-reflection and learning from experience.

Effective leadership development programs can help individuals enhance their potential and become inspiring leaders in their respective fields. These programs often focus on developing the core competencies required for effective leadership, such as strategic thinking, decision-making, conflict resolution, and team building.

Aspiring leaders can also benefit from mentorship programs, where they can learn from experienced leaders and receive valuable guidance in their leadership journey. Additionally, attending conferences, workshops, and networking events related to leadership can provide opportunities for learning, growth, and building a strong support network.

Another crucial aspect of leadership development is understanding the importance of diversity and inclusion. Being an inclusive leader means creating an environment where everyone's voices are heard and valued, regardless of their background, race, gender, or beliefs. And then, being able to manage uncomfortable conversations and comments which can come from this inclusion. This not only fosters a positive work culture but also allows for diverse perspectives and ideas to be considered.

It is worth noting that leadership development should not be limited to just those in formal leadership positions. In fact, every individual has the potential to be a leader in their own way, whether it be through leading a team, taking initiative on projects, or simply setting a good example for others to follow.

Chapter Tips:
1) Create a strong team and make necessary changes when needed.
2) Let those go that don't align with the company's mission.
3) Invest in your people with training/development.
4) Commit to diversity and inclusion on your teams at all levels of the organization. Ensure it reflects those who you are serving, especially at the C-Suite level.

Villa of Hope - Portraits of Hope Gala - 75th Anniversary

7

STRATEGIC TRANSFORMATION & DIVERSITY, EQUITY, INCLUSION, AND BELONGING

We began discussing our next strategic transformation around 2015, when Social Determinants of Health started gaining evidence in research. In fact, research has shown that at least 80% of our physical health is influenced by social determinants. These refer to conditions in which people are born, grow, work, live, and age. This realization led us to focus on addressing Social Determinants of Health directly. We understood that addressing behavioral health concerns was essential, but there were prerequisites for individuals to tackle social determinants, such as finding employment and accessing necessary services. In fact, the Villa was in a strong position to be a leader in this work, and now was that time.

Racism negatively impacts all of the social determinants of health for the Black community

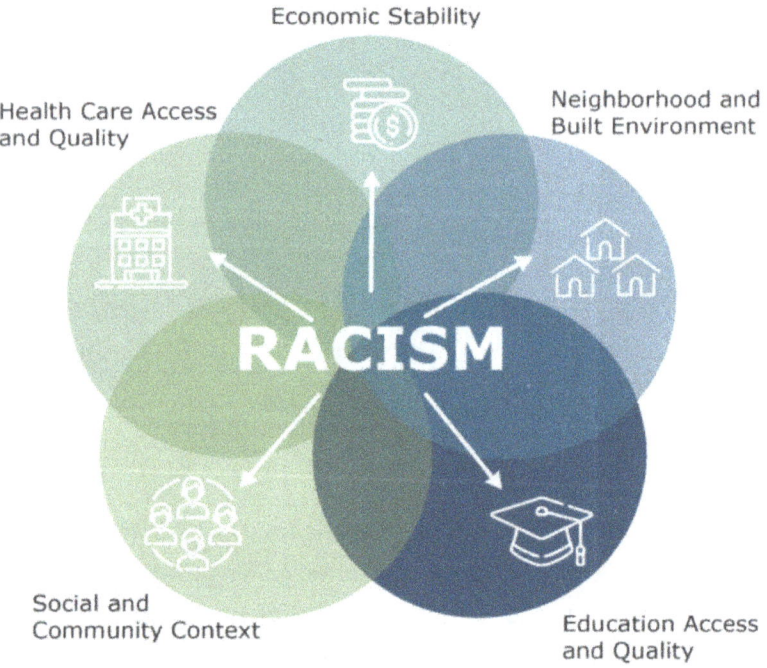

During the Great Migration, Rochester NY went from having around 5,000 people of color in 1910 to almost 30,000 in 1970. Yet, Rochester has a long history of racist policies and practices including refusal to hire people of color, redlining, denials of apartment rentals, restrictive covenants in housing deeds, and exclusionary zoning practices. In fact, out of all 50 states in the U.S.A., the most racially segregated school district border divides Rochester, NY from Penfield NY (based on average levels). Even though data shows that students perform best when classrooms are more diverse. In addition, the average life expectancy of someone within the poorest economic zip code of Rochester (14608) vs. the wealthiest town of Pittsford (14534) is 72.4 years vs. 81.1 years of age. This data comes from a study completed by *Common Ground Health.*

Given this significantly important history of Rochester and the knowledge regarding the impact of Social Determinants of Health on our neighbors, especially our black and brown neighbors, we evolved our next iteration of our vision/direction.

Our Vision 2030 became: *Villa of Hope will advance equity by transforming the social foundations of our neighbors, elevating lifelong health outcomes for our community.*

Our strategy incorporated more focus on changing the fundamentals leading to better health outcomes, continuing to serve children, youth adults and families and expanding our efforts to serve more individuals as well. As a result of this focus, The Villa continued to reduce residential beds and services due to a lack of demand and low daily rates.

Diversity, Equity, Inclusion, and Belonging (D, E, I, B)

More often than not, this journey brought us back to the issue of systemic racism and institutional racism, the impact which was an eye-opening experience earlier in my career when I was out in the community. Institutional racism refers to the systematic discrimination against certain groups of people based on their race, ethnicity, gender, or other characteristics. It is often embedded in policies and practices of institutions such as non-profit organizations, businesses, etc. This results in unequal opportunities and treatment for marginalized groups. We realized that for black and brown community members, the challenges related to social determinants of health were compounded by systemic oppression based on their place in the system (see above graphic). In response, we began another round of education and integration of diversity, equity, inclusion, and belonging initiatives in 2015. Again, it meant finding a professional to partner with to move this forward. We began with internal educational and training sessions until we started an RFP process for a D, E, I, B consultant.

In terms of our Mission and Vision, it was key to understand that black and brown people who are our clients not only faced social determinants of health issues, but also systemic racism and oppression, creating additional layers of challenges. This was met with mixed reactions within our organization. While some fully embraced it, others distanced themselves. Many white individuals had difficulty acknowledging these issues and facts.

To address this, I collaborated with experts from MPG Consulting, who specialize in diversity and inclusion. This group always includes both people of color and white individuals in their work, which I found effective. MPG Consulting helps organizations develop systems for change by exploring the impact of institutional racism, implicit bias, and how to dismantle barriers to workplace success.

I selected 50 people from across our organization, participated myself, and conducted a three-day off-site workshop where we delved into the history of how we arrived in the United States and how our existing structures were created. We discussed concepts like ethnicity and race, differences in lived experiences, and engaged in challenging conversations about white supremacy and implicit bias.

This was particularly difficult for white participants, as most had never been educated on these concepts or history before. People of color expressed frustration at often being expected to educate others and emphasized the importance of white individuals doing their own homework. It was an intense three days, leading to some leaving the organization, some expressing disbelief that our agency was having these discussions, and some taking a wait-and-see approach.

However, we remained committed to the process, similar to what we did with The Sanctuary Model℠. We continued with extensive education. First, we focused on establishing a common language around anti racism work so that people could be grounded and communicate effectively. Similarly, investing in a coach for each Executive Team

Member, and myself, was critical as well. In addition to the training, the coaches helped senior staff navigate challenges that emerged as DEIB work was implemented. Additionally, we formed separate affinity groups for white individuals, Hispanic individuals, and BIPOC (Black, Indigenous, and people of color) individuals. Afterward, we brought everyone back together to determine the best way to implement these learnings. Simultaneously, and with MPG Consulting, we worked with the Board in sessions during retreats throughout the year. It is critical to bring your Board along on the same journey as your staff.

At this point, we invested in and hired a Chief Diversity/HR Officer who partnered with me and MPG Consulting, to continue to move our work/strategy forward. This hire added our second diverse C-Suite member.

We reviewed our policies, procedures, and practices and discovered outdated and discriminatory aspects that we hadn't previously recognized. For instance, our tuition reimbursement plan required upfront payment for courses, which was impractical for our direct care staff earning $16-$17 per hour. We also looked at the percentages of Black, Indigenous, and people of color (BIPOC) individuals in our organization, particularly in management roles, with the goal of shifting these percentages. In essence, this journey was profoundly eye-opening and transformative for our organization.

Honoring the Past and Looking to the Future

In order to add DEIB (Diversity, Equity, Inclusion, and Belonging) into the company, it was essential to acknowledge and address any existing institutional racism within the organization. This meant critically examining hiring practices, promotion processes, and overall workplace culture to identify any biases or barriers that may exist. Furthermore, DEIB should be integrated into all aspects of the company's operations and decision-making processes. This includes hiring, orientation and onboarding, diversity in leadership roles, Board membership, inclusive policies and procedures, and ongoing mandatory education and training for employees on topics such as unconscious bias.

Institutional racism is a deeply rooted construct that needs to be addressed in order to truly achieve diversity, equity, inclusion, and belonging in the workplace. By acknowledging its existence and actively working towards dismantling it, companies can create a more equitable and inclusive environment for not only employees, but also for clients/customers as well. In addition, this important work not only benefits the company itself, but also contributes to creating a more just society overall. It is an ongoing process that requires dedication and continuous evaluation, but the impact of promoting DEIB is invaluable.

At this point in my career, I felt really good. We started turning a profit, had a formal Sanctuary Certification, were working on diversity, equity, inclusion, and belonging initiatives and providing improved services to clients.

Meanwhile, the Villa continued expanding outpatient mental health and community-based programs, including workforce development. Additionally, in 2018 The Villa was awarded a $2.4 million dollar award to build a new detox facility. We were seeing the fruits of seven years of difficult changes and transformation, and it felt great. My plan was to continue to execute, improve upon processes and begin to plan my next steps as we were approaching my ten-year mark. Ten years had always been my soft goal for how long I was going to stay in my CEO role.

And then a pandemic arrived.

Chapter Tips:
1) Implement Diversity, Equity Inclusion & Belonging Initiatives – do your own work first!
2) Include and educate your Board in the same work.
3) Evolve the strategy to meet current situations.
4) Get to reality quick.

During COVID, Villa of Hope ran the first live televised Gala.

8

LEADING THROUGH A PANDEMIC

In 2010, when I accepted the President/CEO role, I quickly knew that it would take 5-10 years to accomplish a transformation. I also didn't want to be a leader that stays for 25 years and loses perspective and/or excitement. Therefore, a 10-year stint from 2010 – 2020 felt about right to me.

Then, our world stopped when the COVID pandemic happened in March of 2020. At this point, I felt I couldn't leave the organization, there were so many unknowns, staff were scared, how we did our work changed and now more than ever, a calm presence was needed.

And if leading through a pandemic was not enough, my dad also died by suicide in September 2020, leaving me responsible for his estate including 15 rental houses with 35 tenants, a Storage Unit business, and his and my grandparent's home. Needless to say, there was a lot on my plate.

The COVID-19 pandemic has been one of the most challenging and unprecedented times in recent history. The outbreak of this novel coronavirus, first identified in Wuhan, China in December 2019, quickly spread to become a global health crisis.

As the virus continued to spread rapidly across continents, governments and organizations around the world were forced to implement strict measures to curb its spread. These included lockdowns, travel restrictions, and social distancing guidelines.

Despite these efforts, the pandemic has continued to wreak havoc on economies, healthcare systems, and communities worldwide. Globally, as of October 2023, there have been 771,407,825 confirmed cases of COVID-19, including 6,972,152 deaths, reported to WHO.

Back then, when it first started, no one knew much about COVID-19 except that many people were dying from it. And now we were asking our direct care staff who only made about $16-$17 per hour to still come into the physical residential programs to work with young people. It was a scene not unlike a hospital unit, with gloves, gowns, and masks. Thankfully, in December 2019, when there was the beginning talks of COVID-19, my team talked through the worst-case scenarios. We made my office the war room and prepared for these potential circumstances. We bought equipment (laptops for remote work, thermometers, gowns, masks, gloves). We sent everybody home with laptops that we could and converted our offices to space we needed. It was good that we prepared in advance, because when we did go into lockdown, we could pivot quickly and not wait for supplies (others were facing long backorders). We had all the supplies necessary because we already planned for the worst case, and here it was.

The Day New York Shut Down

March 22, 2020, was the day NYC officially went into lockdown. The virus entered an exponential growth stage. At the time, the city's infection rate was five times higher than the rest of the country, and its cases were one-third of total confirmed US cases. On March 27th, Queens was the worst-affected borough by number of deaths, with over a third of total deaths. Refrigerator trucks were set up on city streets outside hospitals to accommodate the overflow of bodies of the deceased.

With the onset of the global pandemic caused by the coronavirus, many countries implemented lockdown measures to curb the spread of the virus. The lockdowns resulted in a significant impact on businesses and individuals alike. One of the main concerns for individuals during the lockdowns was determining whether their work was considered essential or not.

Essential work refers to jobs that are deemed critical and necessary during times of crisis, such as a pandemic. These jobs play a crucial role in maintaining the functioning of society and providing essential goods and services to the public. Some examples of essential work include healthcare workers, grocery store employees, first responders, and sanitation workers.

When New York shut down, we determined that we were essential and would remain open. The focus shifted to keeping people safe. Some aspects were relatively straightforward such as implementing policies and understanding telehealth regulations. We still had staff do home visits. Mental health became a major concern, and we organized webinars on topics about working from home and setting up home offices, things we never had to address before.

Keeping Doors Open Through Fear

The whole time, we were working through our own personal fears while adjusting and transforming our technology and services. We communicated via Zoom with our leadership team every morning at 8 A.M. about any new information we heard, concerns they were hearing, supplies needed, or policies we had not thought of, such as having guests coming on campus. In addition, we held Zoom Town Hall meetings once a week to communicate with all staff and answer questions.

Since we were working with the general population, we were putting ourselves and our team at risk of getting COVID-19. So, we had to have testing available to know when someone was positive to contain infection as much as possible. We partnered with the health department, and trained our nursing staff to administer the tests, which allowed us to speed up the testing process, so we received results in less than 24 hours. Still, we had positive cases, and I was with my HR leader making phone calls to staff who had worked with coworkers or youth that tested positive for COVID-19. There were many phone calls where I feared for people, cried for people and their family. It was a horrible message to deliver, but I couldn't make my team member make those calls by herself. I felt a strong sense of responsibility for all 400 employees and our clients. We spent money putting staff up in hotel rooms to isolate them, if they did test positive, so they wouldn't have to go home and put their families at risk. Although we had people hospitalized, thankfully, we didn't have anyone pass away from COVID-19.

With the shutdowns, people who hadn't had mental health issues until now were really struggling, and some turned to substance use. We were seeing a shift in our typical client in our detox facility. During the pandemic, we saw more white males in their 30s. The uncertainty of the pandemic caused heightened mental health needs. Our usual strategic planning took a back seat and my team, and I came into the office every day to address concerns and implement new procedures. We believed that if some staff had to be there, they needed to see our faces. The toughest part was ensuring that employees who had to work directly with clients in residential were compensated adequately.

We received two rounds of the Paycheck Protection Program (PPP) funding that were passed on to the staff for incentive pay, used for necessary equipment, and to cover hotel expenses for some staff. It was a matter of leading through uncharted territory, dealing with the unknown, and making the best decisions in the moment with the information we had and then maintaining clear communication.

The PPP was established in the United States in response to the economic impact of COVID-19. It is a loan program that provides assistance to small businesses, self-employed individuals, and independent contractors who have been affected by the pandemic. The PPP was first signed into law on March 27, 2020, as part of the Coronavirus Aid, Relief, and Economic Security (CARES) Act, and it has since been extended and revised multiple times. This has helped businesses retain their employees and continue operating during the economic downturn.

Our own education programs (grades 7-12) had to go remote. We saw firsthand how our students and parents were affected. I believe we'll see the lasting impacts on their social and emotional development for years to come. They missed out on crucial growth experiences, and everything became centered around technology.

During this time, we saw some significant program funding from the state of New York that stopped due to COVID-19. We went from generating a surplus to losing about $5 million in revenue during the COVID-19 pandemic. Thankfully, we had PPP money to help keep staff employed. We knew it would take time to replace that revenue with behavioral health revenue because the rates are much higher in residential than in Medicaid and billable services.

By the end of 2021, as our heads rose above the chaos and emergency of a pandemic, it was time to address the changes, the loss of funding and what the Villa would look like on the other side of this new normal. This situational strategy process was straightforward and back to basics:

Step 1:
- Review all programs for accurate revenue and expenses.
- Delineate all programs that break even or produce a surplus.
- For programs that can't break even: if there is not a path to

survive on their own, then we are responsible to address it through transfer or closure.

Step 2:
- Review what programs remain and what the path is to get us to Vision 2030 (our long-range strategic plan).
- Decide what the CORE programs are to move to Vision 2030 quickly (CORE programs include direct impacts on social determinants of health factors, or they support a CORE program and themselves and run without a deficit).

Step 3:
- Decide which programs are "non-core" – divest or find the "right" partner.

Step 4:
- Develop organizational structure to execute on Vision 2030.
- Create FY 22-23 Budget.
- Continue possible partnership conversations.

❖ You need to be operationally sustainable, or the Vision does not matter! No margin, no mission.

It was clear we could not stay in evaluation long within the rapidly changing environmental conditions. If Villa did not redesign now, it would not be relevant or even in existence.

As one can imagine, the conversations and the process with all the senior leaders in the organization were difficult. Once again, brutal facts are tough to hear, but as I said to the Executive and Operational team, being at the leadership table means dealing with the discomfort of leadership conversations. It's easy to lead in the good times; it is hard to lead in the tough times. This defines good leaders and organizations from great leaders and organizations.

Chapter Tips:
1) Prepare in advance of crisis – plan for the worst, hope for the best.
2) Communication. Communication. Communication.
3) Bring calmness in chaos.

Social Media post during COVID

My last day and tour of a new renovated building on campus.

9

DECIDING WHEN TO EXIT

I started having some conversations with the Executive Committee about a year in advance of my planned resignation and departure because I knew I would need to give a formal notice six months prior. My daughter was graduating from high school, and I had been working for this agency and in this position since she was five. After sacrificing some things throughout this tenure, I wanted time to enjoy her last bit of senior year and help her figure out her transition plan such as college, trades, military, or work. I wanted to be there for her and spend special quality time during this critical and stressful period. I had also seen the Villa through a strategic transformation and a pandemic. My season was coming to a close, and it was time for new leadership to take the reins, and time for me to take a breath. It was hard to let go because I had invested over 12 years in this organization, but I knew it wasn't in my control anymore.

If you're used to working, when you don't work, you feel guilty for not working anymore. I had to give myself permission and grace to walk away when I knew it wasn't good for me anymore.

Communicating with the Board

The Executive Committee wasn't surprised with my intent to leave because I had discussed it with them. The Board was shocked, but I had never committed to staying for 25 years. My team understood my decision. I had individual conversations with each of them over the previous year. We took proactive steps, such as hiring a search firm and having our Chief Diversity/HR Chief participate on the search team. The Board and I personally engaged with the staff, conducting town hall meetings to address their concerns and questions. Additionally, we conducted a survey and held focus groups that highlighted the importance of culture, open communication, sanctuary, and diversity, equity, inclusion, and belonging, which were the areas staff felt the next CEO needed to possess.

Succession Planning

I didn't want to leave without a clear strategic plan in place. We had job descriptions and profiles that emphasized culture and anti-racism work. I believed I had a solid succession plan in place, initially with two potential successors. We completed necessary tasks, such as compensation analysis in compliance with New York's transparency law. We reviewed and updated our policies, procedures, and practices during our Council of Accreditation certification process.

Everything was well established when I left. My only disappointment was that the financial situation wasn't as strong as I had hoped it would be. However, right before I left in April 2023, we held a Board Retreat where outside speakers joined, specific strategic initiatives were agreed to, a plan of action decided, and a goal to increase revenue was in place.

Deciding when to leave as CEO is a complex and multifaceted decision. As the leader of a company, the responsibility falls on you to determine when it is time to step down from your role. This can be for various reasons, including personal, financial, or strategic considerations.

If the company is thriving under your leadership, you may feel more inclined to stay on as CEO. However, if the company is struggling or facing challenges, you may feel the need to step down and allow someone else to take the reins.

Personal reasons such as health issues or family obligations can also play a role in the decision to leave as CEO. If your physical or mental well-being is being compromised by the demands of the job, it may be time to prioritize your own self-care and step down from your position.

When is it time to go? You should ask yourself these questions:
- Am I here for the title? Is my image and ego tied up in the position?
- Do I still have the passion and energy?
- Is retaining this position about money or retirement?
- Are you genuinely adding value to the organization?
- Are you the right person to execute the next vision and direction?
- Do I represent the population we serve?

Comfort and ego can be powerful factors, and people might stick around because it's what they know, but not what truly drives them. As a CEO, you have the responsibility to not only lead the company but also take care of yourself. It is crucial to listen to your inner voice and trust your instincts when it comes to making this important decision.

Stepping down does not mean failure or weakness, but rather a courageous act of prioritizing what truly matters in life and opening opportunities for the organization you have cared about. Remember that as leaders, we are a steward of the organization for only a period of time.

Transformational Change

By the time I left the Villa of Hope in April of 2023, we no longer had funding from OCFS (Office of Children and Family services), and we had exited all residential programs. At the same time, we had continued to expand to serve adults, as well as families in four core areas and in alignment with our CORE definition: inpatient and outpatient behavioral health (mental health and substance use), community-based programs, workforce development, and care coordination services.

Over the last 12 years, we completely transformed the organization, experienced growth, lived through a pandemic and still went from serving 2,000 clients to 4,000. The percentages of the funding had shifted from 70% Kids Residential to 50% Behavioral Health, 15% Education, and 35% Community and Work Force Development

We had opened the first Inpatient Detox program for youth and adults, expanded the Outpatient Clinic with a second location, and began to look at repurposing residential cottages for affordable housing. Although the organization had around a $1 million deficit, the Villa had the PPP money to cover it. The Villa leadership and Board needed to focus on programs with deficits, execute on strategic priorities established, and seek formal alignments where possible for the future and finding the right next leader.

Chapter Tips:
1) Check your ego – your identity is not your role.
2) Knowing when to exit.
3) Tie up loose ends and support the process.
4) Let go of any decision making around hiring a CEO, that is a Board decision.

My Dad and I working a Gullo Self Storage auction.

10

MY FATHER'S STORY

Since my 20s, I have been very aware of mental health. I have my bachelor's in psychology and master's in social work. The definition of mental health for every one of us is our emotional, psychological, and social well-being. It affects how we think, how we feel, how we act, and it determines how we handle stress, how we relate to others, and how we make healthy choices; something we all hope to master in a positive way. Today through research we know there are even more factors that have a huge impact on mental health; grief, loss, trauma events, the news, the COVID-19 pandemic, social media, especially for adolescents. Some of us work through these experiences, using tools such as therapy, self-care, etc. Others become ill and develop diagnoses of depression, anxiety, panic attacks, and the need for treatment.

Early in my tenure at Villa of Hope, mental health and mental illness were quickly moving to the forefront of both national and community need. Although I could share many stories from the people at the Villa, I'm here to share with you a very personal story about mental health. A story of one man's journey, the upside, the challenges, the joy.

The story is about my dad, Frank Gullo Jr. Little Frankie as he was called in our family. He was born on November 19, 1949, in Sonyea, New York. He was the oldest of three brothers, and as the oldest, he was always the responsible one. In fact, he spent a lot of his childhood with his grandfather and uncle on the farm down the road, learning the responsibilities of working the field that I would experience in my own childhood. He loved learning about farming, feeding the calves, driving equipment. He even bought his own car at 16.

After graduating from high school, my parents were married at the age of 18. My grandparents sold them a piece of property on the same road next-door to them. They put a trailer on the lot and my dad began designing their home. He was an amazing carpenter, and he could build just about anything in his head. He would draw it on paper and then bring it to life, this talent I did not inherit at all.

After high school he worked during the day and attended school in Rochester in the evening for his apprenticeship and carpenter training. When he completed that program in 1972, he opened his own contracting business and by the time I was five we had moved into a beautiful ranch my dad built with the help of many of his uncles. He loved that house, and he took great pride in the fact that he built it with his own hands.

My dad's contracting business was successful. He was well trusted and respected in our area, but the love of farming ran deep into his blood. So, in addition to his contracting business, in his 20s, he purchased a small farm and land from a neighbor that was retiring from the farming business. Gullo Farms eventually grew to include beef cattle, pigs, crops, and equipment.

For 25 years, my dad worked seven days a week, very long days, and did so because he absolutely loved it. It was his passion. The time I spent with my dad until I was 18 consisted of feeding the calves, baling, and stacking the hay, learning how to drive a tractor, chopping wood, building a deck for a swimming pool, learning to play poker, shoot pool, and the ongoing car maintenance lessons that he felt were so important, especially for women to know.

During this time together, he more than once provided one piece of advice over and over, "Whatever you do, you want to be able to take care of yourself. Do not depend on someone else to provide for you."

Work certainly was my dad 's purpose, and he loved it!

In his 50s, he underwent a major surgery that permanently prevented him from heavy lifting. He had to give up his contracting business and his farm. As he watched the beef cattle and equipment being sold, he became more and more depressed. He would get up in the morning hardly eat, head to the couch for the rest of the day, go to bed and do it all over again the next day. During this time, with my social work degree, I was able to talk with him about mental health and depression. He finally agreed to see a therapist. He carried a deep amount of grief, lack of purpose and guilt. Similar to many of us, he also had childhood pain and events that he never talked about before. Thankfully, the treatment and one on one counseling appointments addressed these issues. With finding the right medication, it opened the space for dad to find new purpose.

In '95, he did a lot of reading about a new concept of self-storage businesses. My dad was always an entrepreneur. He had the land, so he decided to build one storage building of 30 units. Demand took off quickly, so he added more, eventually growing to 90 units which he incorporated as Gullo Self-Storage Inc. Additionally, he also began investing in real estate and rental properties, resulting in a total of 13 houses with 30+ tenants, which created Gullo Properties, LLC.

Over a decade, he had built two new businesses and was a well-respected property owner and business-person. He was known for doing the right thing sometimes to his own disservice. Like allowing people to remain without paying rent or waiving security deposits.

During this time my dad would continue to access mental health treatment as needed and continued his medication. Through his counseling work, he decided to separate from my mom in 2018 after 50 years of marriage. But it was not until two years later in March 2020, that the separation agreement was finally complete.

Those COVID-19 years took a toll for many, and the number of diagnosed cases of anxiety and depression surged. A positive thing that came from COVID-19 is that we have seen both the local and national awareness develop around the impacts of mental health, alcohol and drug use, and the services available. Researchers are clear that the next pandemic is a mental health one.

In early 2020, I was enveloped in heightened awareness of mental health. It was always on my mind concerning our Villa staff, our clients, my own daughter in high school, my dad's mental health, as well as my own. During this time, my dad and I had many conversations about his grief and loss, the legal challenges he was facing with the divorce and selling the properties, his feelings of depression and being overwhelmed, and to a large extent, confusion as to what his sense of purpose was. After all of this, he was now facing the possibility of needing to sell Gullo Self-Storage Inc. He would lose the Homestead house of my grandparents and the house he had built. These possibilities weighed heavy on him, and it was devastating for him to think about all this happening on his watch. A mile-long stretch of Ridge Road in Mt. Morris had been in his family for decades. Generations of family had farmed, including himself, and the Homestead house of my great grandparents was still there along with the storage business and the house my dad designed and built, the house I was raised.

From April through September 2020, I watched and listened as my dad struggled to keep everything going. He fell behind on the maintenance of some rental properties, returning calls, and completing taxes. I watched as he lost energy to do things, he slept a lot, and he carried a great deal of stress. Mental health treatment and counseling continued. Meds were working and a safety plan was set in place, and I was at the top of that list. He was 71 and although he adored his family, especially my daughter, his only granddaughter, it was all too much.

Right after Labor Day weekend on September 8, 2020 as I was wrapping up my last conference call of the day, my dad's girlfriend called me to say that he had left her apartment that morning and she had not seen him since. He had not answered his cell phone all day. Immediately, I had a bad gut feeling. I called his cell as he would always pick up for me, but no answer. In the meantime, his girlfriend drove to his house, and there was his truck, but no answer at the door. I knew we needed to call 911.

For the next two hours, I prepared myself for the news I already knew was coming. He had died by suicide from a self-inflicted gunshot wound.

Over the course of that evening, I needed to tell my then 15-year-old daughter, that her papa had passed. I will never forget that conversation. I shared with her whatever she asked, whatever she wanted to know. I believe a big piece of our healing is understanding, and for each of us, that level of understanding in the details is likely different for each person. There is no wrong answer. There are only individual answers.

As his only child, I had to quickly begin to get my arms around where all the rental properties were, who the tenants were, where he was in the selling process, learning how to run a storage business and figuring out how to complete the many needed steps in the separation agreement. He did everything on paper and what was not on a Post-it note, he stored in his head.

It did not take long for me to see his intentional planning. My dad had deliberately done things to help me in the short term. His final gift from him to me; he had paid all mortgage payments two months in advance to buy time for me to figure things out, all upcoming bills had been paid and he completed his taxes and dropped them off to the accountant just that morning the day he died by suicide. Although he could not carry this work forward himself, he wanted to make it easier for me. There is no question my dad knew the enormity of the work he was leaving me. He also knew I was smart and committed. After all, I am his daughter through and through.

It took almost 3 years to close the Estate, from organizing, meeting tenants, selling properties, cleaning out his house and finally, selling Ridge Road properties. It has been extremely frustrating, bittersweet and heart wrenching. I can totally understand what he was seeing and feeling from his perspective, and I also know my husband and I saw through what he could not. So many times, a tenant would say, "Your dad was the best landlord, he was a great guy." "He did this for me, or he did that for me." "I rented from him for years." He was very proud of all he accomplished, and how he treated people, and his granddaughter Alex was the light of his life.

Obviously, this is not the way I would have wanted my dad's life to come to a close, but that is also not my choice. We do not walk in other shoes. All we can do is try our best to understand. He did everything he could do for himself, his businesses, his tenants, and for myself and Alex. I know he thought long and hard about his decision. That's how he made every decision, and I know it was not an easy choice, and yet for him it was a choice on his terms, his time, at his place.

I hope this will position all of you to be helpful if you need to support someone who is struggling with a mental health challenge. Awareness and eliminating stigma around mental health and addiction is critical. We must talk about it and there should not be shame in it. This has been a positive of the pandemic. Ask someone if they are okay, if you can help – tell them, treatment is good, get them connected.

Mental health illness is the same as any other. Like cancer, symptoms appear, diagnosis happens, treatment takes place and hopefully, allows for the gift of time. Some much longer than others, but boy are we grateful for that gift of time.

From my dad 's initial diagnosis and treatment, he got another 20+ years. Which means I had that many more talks and laughs with my dad. He saw my daughter being born and was a big part of her life. He impacted many other lives. He was at my wedding to my husband and saw our house built. He attended many Villa events, and he was a really proud dad. We told each other I love you through visits, phone calls or texts.

I have no regrets. Do not have regrets, tell people you love them. And when mental health – addiction (a disease just like cancer) occurs, and loss happens – we need our own mental health support – and that is not weakness. It is to provide self-care, a place to grieve, process, move forward and be among the living. I know that is what my dad would want. I carry my dad with me every day, I hear from him often, and I represent all he stood for.

My parents, John and I at our wedding.

Chapter Tips:
1) Ask people if they are okay.
2) Work to remove the stigma of mental health.
3) Don't have regrets – say what you need and want – tell people you love them.

Out of the Darkness Walk, in honor of my dad. John, Alex and I with my stepkids (Shannon and Patrick) and their significant others (Justin and Robbie) and Shannon and Justin's kids - Weston & Harry.

FINAL THOUGHTS

Leadership development is a forever journey and must come from the inside. You have to have a healthy ego, self-awareness, emotional intelligence, and appropriate vulnerability. I don't think a leader without those things could comfortably or successfully do what I did. Also, you don't have to have all the answers and know everything. It's okay to admit that you need help. People are willing and want to help.

As an organization, it is critical to have a set of guiding principles, as it provides a foundation for expectations and how to behave. As a leader, you must have a strategy and must put the right people in the right seats with the right skill sets around you, and then execute. In fact, I like surrounding myself with people who are smarter and different than me because you get unique perspectives and can arrive at better decisions. If you are in a not-for-profit organization, remember that it is a business, and you need to run it like a business.

It takes courage to have hard conversations that lead to development. It takes courage to face brutal facts, share them, and begin to move forward. Repeatedly though, research and surveys tell us that employees want to be told the truth. This means being open, honest, direct, and timely. Employees deserve the truth; it is the most humane course and it's the prime responsibility of a leader to have managerial courage to tell the truth, show a path forward, and then to act.

Last, don't take yourself too seriously. Laugh at yourself. Be authentic and courageous, and know when it's your time to exit stage right.

Although I talk through many examples of what worked well, there were many trials and errors and mistakes along the way. Failures are important, they make us better by failing forward. Best advice is to fail fast, learn from it, and move on quickly. If you are not proactively making changes to improve things or your unhappy with the results, you forfeit the right to complain about them.

It is very powerful for staff to see failures and mistakes. When they happened, I owned them, communicated it and changed/adjusted course. Seeing a leader do this provides for the safety of our staff to take risks and learn from failures. In the end, the entire organization is better!

Finally, in reflecting on the chapter takeaways, the following are my top 10 leadership values I strive to live by:

1) Take risks and follow your gut.
2) Deliver hard news yourself.
3) Get clear on mission & vision and set a strategy plan – be inclusive.
4) Most times, the hardest thing and the right thing are the same.
5) Establish company values & Guiding Principles and embed them in your organization.
6) Commit to diversity and inclusion on your teams at all levels of the organization. Ensure it reflects those you are serving, especially at the C-Suite level.
7) Get to reality quick.
8) Bring calmness in chaos.
9) Check your ego – your identity is not your role.
10) Ask people if they are okay.

"Knowing my True North gives me the courage to focus my energy where I believe it should be, not according to what is popular or pleasing to others."

- *Jennifer Cummings*

Reference Page(s):

Adaptive change as a result of confronting the brutal facts | Villa of Hope. (2021, June 30). Villa of Hope. https://www.villaofhope.org/adaptive-change-as-a-result-of-confronting-the-brutal-facts/

COVID-19 cases | WHO COVID-19 dashboard. (n.d.). Datadot. https://data.who.int/dashboards/covid19/cases?n=c

COVID-19 pandemic in New York City. (2024, March 16). Wikipedia. https://en.wikipedia.org/wiki/COVID-19_pandemic_in_New_York_City

Dougherty, Nate. (2013, April 19). *Non-profit erases deficit, adopts new name*. Rochester Business Journal. Non-profit erases deficit, adopts new name - Rochester Business Journal (rbj.net)

Racism is key driver of illness and early death for Black residents, regional study finds | Common Ground Health. (n.d.). Common Ground Health. https://www.commongroundhealth.org/news/articles/racism-is-key-driver-of-illness-and-early-death-for-black-residents-regional-study-finds

King, S. F., Seale, L., & Ross, A. L. *Home - Kros Learning Group*. (2023, September 19). Kros Learning Group. https://kroslearninggroup.com/

Making Strategy Count in the Health and Human Services Sector: Lessons Learned from 20 Organizations and Chief Strategy Officers | eBook. Barnes & Noble. https://www.barnesandnoble.com/w/making-strategy-count-in-the-health-and-human-services-sector-michael-mortell/1136844596

Mary Kay: You Can Have It All: Lifetime Wisdom from America's Foremost Woman Entrepreneur: Ash, Mary Kay: 9780761501626: Amazon.com: Books. (n.d.). https://www.amazon.com/Mary-Kay-Lifetime-Americas-Entrepreneur/dp/0761501622

MPG Consulting. (2022, March 26). *Home - Welcome to Mary Pender Greene, LCSW-R, CGP President and CEO of MPG Consulting*. https://marypendergreene.com/

Villa of Hope: Mental Health & Social Service in Rochester NY. (2023, December 15). Villa of Hope. https://www.villaofhope.org/

Sanctuary Institute – Thinking Globally about kids. (n.d.). Sanctuary Institute. https://www.thesanctuaryinstitute.org/

Smith, I. (2021, September 22). *How does trauma affect the brain? - and what it means for you*. Whole Wellness Therapy. https://www.wholewellnesstherapy.com/post/trauma-and-the-brain

ABOUT THE AUTHOR

Christina M. Gullo grew up in a small town in upstate New York. She currently lives in Webster, NY with her husband, daughter, two shelties and a cat. She loves to cook, exercise, travel and spend time with her adult stepdaughter and son and their family, especially being a Nonna to two young step grandsons. They like spending time in Florida at their condo near West Palm Beach. Being on the water is her happy place.

She has a Bachelors in Psychology, MBA & Masters in Social Work and a SHRM – Senior Professional in HR Certification and Senior Certified Professional.

She can be contacted on her LinkedIn profile:
www.linkedin.com/in/christina-gullo-49135430

www.ingramcontent.com/pod-product-compliance
Lightning Source LLC
Chambersburg PA
CBHW072201100426
42738CB00011BA/2499